For my darling Greylin —

The brightest star in my world,
The inspiration behind every page,
and the reason I believe in big dreams.

Gigi–The Mini Creator

By: Courtney Michelle

Gigi watched with eyes so wide,
As Mommy filmed her day with pride.
With camera up and lights aglow,
She smiled and posed like a pro.

"One day," said Gigi, "I'll do that too!
I've got big dreams—and ideas too!"
She grabbed her toys, her glittery case,
And set up shop all over the place.

4

She made a stand with blocks and tape,
Her teddy bear wore a superhero cape.
With a spoon and a pot in her hands—
"Today we're cooking snacks!" she said.

“Hello friends, I’m Gigi the star,
I make big shows, right where we are!
We’re mixing snacks with fruit and crunch,
Let’s stir it up and eat some lunch!”

She danced, she twirled, she sang with flair,
Tried on sunglasses and brushed her hair.
She gave a talk on how to shine,
Then spilled some juice—“Oh no, it’s mine!”

She stomped her foot and gave a sigh,
"This doesn't work—I didn't try!"
But Mommy smiled and knelt down low,
"There's something you should really know..."

“The best creators try and play,
They laugh, they learn along the way.
It’s not about a perfect take—
Mistakes are what real stars make!”

"You don't need fans or fancy views,
To share your voice or wear cool shoes.
Just have some fun, be brave, be you—
There's nothing more you have to do."

Gigi beamed, her heart felt light,
She giggled hard and held Mom tight.
"Then I'll keep playing, loud and proud—
I'll be a star without a crowd!"

So every day she danced and made,
With cardboard sets and dress-up shades.
A mini creator, bold and free—
Just Gigi being Gigi... as happy as can be.

HI! I'm Gigi!

Meet Greylin "Gigi"

GIGI IS ALMOST THREE YEARS OLD, FULL OF SPARKLE, AND ALWAYS HAS SOMETHING TO SAY!

SHE LOVESSSSS TO PLAY DRESS UP, STRIKE A POSE, AND CREATE HER OWN SHOWS.

WHEN SHE'S NOT PRETENDING TO FILM, SHE'S BUSY PLAYING WITH HER SISTER, DANCING IN HER BALLERINA OUTFITS, OR HELPING HER MOMMY MAKE SNACKS.

Gigi's Favorite Things

COLOR: PINK WITH SPARKLES

SNACK:STRAWBERRIES WITH A LITTLE SUGAR!

HOBBY: DANCING BALLET & FILMING HER OWN PRETEND VIDEOS

SIDEKICK: HER PUPPY NAMED "PRINCESS"

About the Author

Courtney Michelle is a content creator, storyteller, and proud mama to her mini muse, Gigi. With a passion for inspiring the next generation to dream big and express themselves boldly, she wrote this book to celebrate creativity, confidence, and all the magic that comes from simply being you.

Made in the USA
Columbia, SC
29 April 2025

57115912R00018